I0111597

STANDARDS FOR SUCCESS:
FROM THE LIFE OF KING DAVID

By
Terry Shuttlesworth

D C C
INTL

Unless otherwise indicated, all scripture quotations are taken from the King James Version of the Bible.

STANDARDS FOR SUCCESS: From the Life of King David
ISBN 978-0-692-65726-3
Copyright 2005 by Terry Shuttlesworth

Published by Dominion International
Virginia Beach, Virginia 23456

Printed in the United States of America.
All rights reserved under International Copyright Law.
Contents and/or cover may not be reproduced in whole or in part in any form without the express written consent of the publisher.

DEDICATION

I would like to dedicate this book to my best friend and closest confidant. It has been her inspiration and grit that have encouraged me time and again. She has taught me the art of consistency and raw determination. If one is to have an armor bearer, then she is mine. I dedicate this book to my wife . . . Colleen.

CONTENTS

FOREWORD

The life of David is as exciting as it is revealing. Terry holds you by the hand and leads you through the corridors of David's childhood, the cornfields where David walked, and the star-filled nights of the lonely shepherd boy guarding his sheep, all the way to the sounds of Israel's victorious battle cries. Terry takes us to the well, escorts us to the dayspring and shows us David's adoration of God through the soothing tones of the harp. Our journey takes us to the dark valley of David's fleshly weakness and back again to the reverberating clash of spears and shields.

Terry gives a narration of the life and times of David in the most lucid form. He writes in a manner that only a man who has the same well as King David can write. I have known Terry for over 15 years, sometimes at close range. I have witnessed the growth and blessing of his ministry. Terry has a message for this generation and I recommend this book highly.

Standards for Success is the book that this generation has been waiting for without knowing it. It is my belief that your individual desire is to be successful. However, you must understand that desire on its own is never enough. God's standards exist for anyone who desires success in life and ministry. This book has been masterfully written so that great nuggets of truth are unveiled and precious gems are unearthed. Like a painter, Terry throws light and dazzling splashes of color on the canvas of the past. He hands us a picture of a prophet, a priest, and a king: the servant of God, the man David.

Turn the pages in expectation; the next turn will be the right one. It is the turn you have trusted the Lord for in your walk with Christ. This turn might start you on a journey that you have never walked before. Saddle up your horses; get ready to go up to the next level.

This book is timely, as God is searching today for Davids to stand for Him. The mouths of Goliaths have to be stopped, and the challenges and taunts of the devil have to be checked. Bickering from within has to cease. In my thirty-three years of ministry, I have taught and counseled young ministers of the gospel on important issues of humility and respect for the anointing. It is reassuring to see Terry unveil similar truths in this book. If ever there was a time that God needed a David, it is now in these end times. You might be that David. Rise up from the shackles of your past and be counted.

Pastor Ayo Oritsejafor
30,000 member; Word of Life Bible Church
Warri, Nigeria

PREFACE

It is my distinct pleasure to endorse Standards for Success, a unique look into the life of David by Dr. Terry Shuttlesworth. He uses the life of one of the greatest men of God in the Old Testament, King David, as his backdrop. He traces his steps from the time of his anointing, to the time God established his kingdom on the throne of Israel.

Anyone called of God will appreciate this study in the life of David, the man after God's own heart. Before David ascended to the throne as king over the entire nation of Israel, there was much that befell him which could have caused him great doubt. He was rejected, pursued by Saul, and he became the companion of fugitives. Those who stayed with him eventually became the aristocracy of Israel. Yes, David had failures—but he came back, and he was restored to the place from which he had fallen. The best part about the story is that from his lineage the Savior came, and Jesus of Nazareth was called the "Son of David". What a victory story!

You will have to read the book to get the full impact of this important message. While you are at it, pick up several copies because you will want to share this book with your family and friends. You can become the missionary who restores someone else back to ministry!

I've known the Shuttlesworth family for many years. They are preaching the Gospel of Jesus Christ today with the demonstration of power. It is my honor to recommend Terry's great book, Standards for Success.

R.W. Schambach
Evangelist/Friend
Founder of Schambach Ministries

THE APPEAL OF DAVID

What is it about King David that everyone seems to be drawn to? Is it his charm or charisma? Usually, those are things that are only discerned through personal contact. Maybe it's the excitement of his life, or possibly the prestige and power of the King that magnetizes you to him. Do you associate somehow with the warrior? How about the priest or the prophet? What is it that is so appealing? If you are truthful with yourself as you read this, your answer is most likely that **you are magnetized by this Bible personality because you can identify with <u>the humanity</u> of such an influential figure who had the attention of Jehovah God Himself!**

I wonder if you are the person empowered by David's life because **it inspires you to achieve, even when you are in failure.** It takes a great man or woman to admit that their life is in need of changes, but those are just the people God chooses to use to build His Kingdom. As you read the following pages, there are Biblical principles that will unlock doors into your future and illuminate rooms of opportunity for your life. Let us see what is alive on the inside of you… or what is not. — **T.S.**

CHAPTER ONE

HE WAS ANOINTED BY GOD

The people who were the closest to David prejudiced him the most. You recall the scene don't you? It's found in 1 Samuel 16. The Prophet Samuel had taken a long journey with a ram's horn filled with oil, instead of the water it normally carried for long journeys through desert heat. This was the first indication that **God was ready to supernaturally turn the fate of Israel around,** by removing the people from the manipulation of Saul.

Why do we use the term "manipulation", you may ask? The Bible says that God had "rejected Saul from reigning over Israel." **You cannot presume to lead what is God's, without God's anointed approval to do so.** Saul therefore could not have been properly leading Israel. He had to have been driving them with human powers at best. That is manipulation.

Let's go now to the room where you'll see the anointing taking place. Samuel arrives at Jesse's house and follows God's instruction to offer a sacrifice. He calls Jesse and his sons to the sacrifice and consecrates them to the Lord. Unless you look closely, you will miss the first act of prejudice against David.

What is **prejudice? It is making an incorrect determination before all the facts are known.** The first act of prejudice was made by Jesse, David's own father. Why had he not consecrated David with the other sons? It is a simple deduction. David was not invited to the sacrifice because his father did not feel he had any business there at the time. After all, David is just a young shepherd who should mind the sheep and leave the greater matters to the others. He may not have been old enough to lead Israel at that time, that is true, but **this was not a coronation ceremony, this was an inspiration from God.** No one was being crowned King that day, but a prophet was being raised up from that room, one who would learn to prophesy in isolation with a melody that would be uniquely his own.

The second occurrence of prejudice was from the prophet Samuel. The Bible says that **when Samuel looked** at Eliab, the eldest son of Jesse, he declared that surely this was the Lord's anointed. Eliab is the most mature of all the sons, and after all, this would also follow the precedent of Hebrew tradition. The oldest son should receive the covenant blessing from the father. **Samuel missed God. He was looking for a King in that room, whereas God was looking for a Prophet that would be a King.**

The key into this room is found in the prime directive given to Samuel before he left to go to Jesse's house. It's right there in the very first verse of 1 Samuel 16. God said, "I have provided for **Myself** a King among his sons." Samuel should have known that what **God was looking for was a person who did what God did, and said what God said**—a Prophet . . . **a Prophet who would be Priest, as well as a King.** The Bible declares that Saul was the choice of the people. The difference between Saul and David is simple, **Saul is the people's King and David is God's.**

At the time of this writing, I feel led to tell some of the readers that **you can never get your children in the anointing too early!** Train up the children in the right ways of God and when they get older they will not leave the right ways of God. That is **a promise for your house that must be lived out through a lifetime, not just spoken in a moment.** The Bible indicates that the basis of God's judgment here concerning David was not who was in the room **at that**

time, but what would become of the people who were in that room **in time.** When David was called for and entered the room, the Spirit of God commanded the people in the room to get on their feet; their future King had entered.

We should never assume a position that God has not ordained and anointed us for. It was **a mantle** God gave away that day, **not a scepter.** In 1 Samuel 15 and verse 27 the Bible says that, **"Saul lunged for the skirt of Samuel's mantle and it tore."** Saul had missed his own calling and in desperation was grabbing for another's calling. We must learn a great lesson here. **Thrones are for Kings and Mantles are for Prophets.** Don't touch what doesn't belong to you.

CHAPTER TWO
HE THOUGHT AS THE SHEPHERD

What is on the inside of you, will eventually show up on the outside of you. The Bible is clear when it tells us in the Book of Romans the 4th chapter, that faith is what makes the promises of God sure to the end. **If God starts something, He never lets it go unfinished.** Faith calls the invisible world of the Spirit into the visible world of the flesh.

David had to act on his faith like anyone else. **Believing in God didn't start after Hebrews, Chapter 11 was written.** We know Abraham is considered the Father of faith and is often the drawn comparison of new Testament writings concerning faith. When the Bible teaches us in the new covenant that when God says a thing, He also has the power to make it happen. You know that He has always had that ability. Samuel spoke the Word of the Lord over David, but it was David that had to believe in the God of that Word. **God's performance is on the other side of man's obedience.**

19

The story of David has been misrepresented for years. When David came to the battlefield that day in the Valley of Elah, quite a bit of time had elapsed, and many things had already taken place to the men that had been at the anointing of David in Jesse's house. The 17th chapter of 1 Samuel draws our eye to the time. Verse 12 informs us that Jesse was an old man advanced in years in these days of Saul. Many people skip right over the 16th chapter's end, and go from the anointing of David straight to Goliath. **You must understand the process of the Word of the Lord, to see the performance of it.**

Let's take a look into the preparation of David for a moment. **The key into a private view of the King, for David, was not his winsome look, as much as it was his ability to worship.** We are told that God's spirit is removed from Saul and that he is now a troubled man, tormented by an evil spirit. Saul sent his servants to find him relief through music. The Bible says that one of Saul's servants, who was a *young man,* said that he had **seen a son of Jesse.** To this young man, David stood out among all the sons. Here is our first description of David since Samuel's visit to the house. The servant of Saul describes him in the 18th Verse as a skillful musician, a mighty and violent man, **a man of war,** a man wise in his speaking and affairs, an attractive man, and last but not least, he says that the Lord is with him. **David has matured in his anointing.**

Saul sends his messengers to Jesse and asks him to send him David. The Bible says that Saul became very fond of David and appointed him in the most trustworthy of positions…armor-bearer to the King. David is not a child. I think we must continue **to see the prejudice of his peers and realize that, to an older man, he seems an adolescent, but the description of David given by the young man was anything but that.** David's potential and anointing were measured from the inside by God. He was forming David into what He needed on the earth at that time. What we need to grasp from all of this, is that by the time David went to the battlefield in Elah, he definitely was not a novice. A King does not let a novice in warfare bear his armor. At the time that the battle was going on between Israel and the Philistines, David was traveling back and forth from his father's house to the palace of Saul. David was already an armor-bearer for Saul, and also continued as a shepherd for his father.

The majority of David's preparation, up until this point, has been as a shepherd. What we are seeing now is a transition from that. **The care of the sheep had instilled within**

him a shepherd's heart, one that he would need later in order to understand the nation he would care for. When David arrived at the battle, he is once again challenged in his authority. This time, it is his oldest brother, Eliab, that hears David talking with the men about what is to be done for the man who defeats Goliath.

God is a rewarder of them that diligently seek after Him. David finds out that the man who defeats Goliath is going to be given wealth, the King's oldest daughter, and his house would be free of taxation. When Eliab hears this, he is angry with David. He asks David why he has come down to the battle, and then tries to compensate for his own weakness by asking David who he left the sheep with. Eliab is an angry, jealous man. So angry is Eliab, that he speaks against his own house by saying, "those few sheep". Eliab tells David, "I know why you're here…you came to fight." Is that a bad thing? There is, after all, a battle going at that time. Obviously, the call to battle was not being answered by the others at this point. David replied with something very interesting. David said to Eliab, his brother, "What have I done now?" I think we can clearly draw a conclusion that David has been badgered by Eliab for some time. Why would David have referred to "now" unless there had been other times throughout his life like this, with Eliab? **David**

turned away from Eliab and continued to pursue his divine appointment.

We must keep our eyes focused on our purposes in God, and not be distracted by the emotions of others around us. **When David turned from Eliab that day, he never went back to his father's sheep again.** *Very often in this life, a soulish tie must be broken in order for an individual to move on to the next level of their divine appointment on the earth.* David broke the tie that day that his own brother had on him.

CHAPTER THREE

HE FOUGHT AS THE KING

Who would be a worthy opponent for David? A ten-foot tall giant of a man named Goliath. 1 Samuel 17 is one of the most famous scenes of the entire Bible.

Goliath's coat of mail weighed approximately 126 pounds, his spear the size of a fence rail. The tip of his spear alone weighed 15 pounds. His armor was constructed of solid bronze that included a helmet, his coat of mail, and his leg and shin protection. **It will be your conflicts, in this fight of faith, that will decide your advancements and your adversaries. If you pray to God for a divine purpose, He'll send you to defeat an enemy of the kingdom for Him. After all, how could you be an overcomer without something to overcome.**

If you desire for God to use your life to do what no one else has yet done, then your conflict of faith will be a unique one. **Without a peculiar enemy to conquer, Da-**

vid would just have been one among many! If you are looking for the overcomer's reward, then get ready to define what you have never laid your eyes on before.

God didn't tell David to fight Goliath. *David heard and saw what the enemy of Israel was saying and doing, and it was his courage and faith in God that moved him from his carriage to the battlefield.* When you look closely at Goliath's armor, you see the enemy more clearly. The armor tells you that he is a defender and protector of something. What is he the defender and protector of? Who is the armor on? Is the armor on Philistia or is it on Goliath? The armor is protecting him. Who is he? **He is the embodiment of the harmony between pride and rebellion, a descendant of fallen angels and evil men.** His armor is seen prophetically as incorrect judgment or oppression. **The brass that he bears on his person is only a shell that is empowered by the motives that lie beneath it.**

The spirit that is on the inside of Goliath knows that if it sides with the spirit that is on the inside of Saul, there would be a common pact of surrender. In Chapter 17 and verse 8, Goliath shouts, "Am I not a Philistine, and are you not servants of Saul?" The Bible says he did this for forty days. On the morning of the forty-first day, a servant, who was not of Saul, arrived. The Bible says that Goliath presented himself **40 days.** This **represents a completed cycle of time and the end of something that has generated.** In the opinion of this author, **David arrived on the first day of a new beginning.** You see the fortieth day was the enemy's last day of national victory and the forty-first day was **David's first day of national victory.** This day would be set apart from any other for the rest of his life.

Your similarity will group you with others, your difference will set you apart. David didn't fight Goliath with a burst of energy and a good idea. David had been pre-developed in his courage by God against lions and bears, long before he went up against the giant. **It is only the anointing of God that will bring you the success in God that you need.** Not only is it important that you follow the set race God has deigned specifically for you, but you must combine that with the development and use of your own personal faith and anointing that God has developed specifically for you.

With that in mind, we understand precisely why David took off the armor of Saul and went with what had worked previously for him. God didn't need the methods of Saul here, He needed what was in David. So much has been said through the years about the five stones taken from the brook that day by David. Preachers and teachers have said that the four stones that remained in David's bag were for Goliath's four brothers. I think that is a far stretch of the imagination. I would hold fast to the principle that when you destroy the enemy in your life, make sure you destroy every aspect of the hindrance, or what is not dealt with will rise up another day. I believe what I am getting ready to share with you will shed light on this shaded principle.

David picked up five stones in case he missed. One person may say, that is a simple, brilliant plan. Always have a back up. I think what we must address here is the question of whether this is God's fight or David's. David's words were that the Lord was going to deliver Goliath into his hands. **God doesn't miss.** Not one plan of God has ever failed. Failure is only in man's involvement with the plan of God. **Faith doesn't have a plan B.** A rock and a sling aren't what David needs to complete this exercise of faith. If you read this closely, you will realize the exact moment that **David went from the training of the shepherd into the training of the king.**

I also want you to understand that it was the prophetic anointing he already had in his life that he spoke forth.

David declares in verse 46, that the Lord was going to deliver Goliath into the hands of David and that David was going to cut his head off. **This prophecy required more than a sling and a stone, these are but the weapons of a shepherd.** This prophecy required a peculiar sword, a unique weapon. This Word from the Lord required Goliath's sword. That's why God didn't allow David to take the sword of Saul. The sword that God would put in the hands of David that day would be the finest on the earth. Goliath sword was a prophetic symbol of David's purpose on the earth. It would be the weight and balance of that weapon, which was forged to defeat the people of God, that God would use to defeat a godless people. Can you hear it in your spirit? **No weapon formed against you shall prosper!**

The Bible says that no sword was in David's hand. God will take what the enemy meant to harm you and turn it against him, tipping the scales in your favor. **The stone and the sling are what allowed David to get close, but it was the sword that brought a new dimension into his life.** He started that day as a shepherd but he finished it fighting like a king.

CHAPTER FOUR

HE PRAYED AS THE PRIEST

There have been many books written on the life of David that focus on his development under Saul's oppressing hand, and the relationship he had developed with Jonathan, Saul's son. **It was David's respect for authority that brought him authority.** David sowed many seeds of greatness along the path of his destiny. Not enough can be written about respecting the anointing and the anointed.

What I would like to deal with in this chapter is what I believe David loved the most of all, which were the things God allowed him to have in his life. **David's greatest love was found in David's greatest desire.** David never saw what he would have called his crowning achievement in his lifetime. **David's greatest desire was to build God a house, and that desire was born out of his love to function as the Priest of God.** There are many instances in the scripture where David functioned as priest, but there are two particular occasions that I would like for us to study out together.

The first example is found in the 30th chapter of 1st Samuel. We find David, with his army, returning from battle to their camp at Ziklag. Ziklag has been burned out, and all of their families have been captured by the enemy while they were away. The Bible says that David and his men came back on **the third day.** *I believe this is an old covenant shadow of the third day, referred to by the prophets throughout scriptures.* **"One day is as a thousand years, and a thousand years is as one day."** While this is imperfect in representation, it still must be viewed in light of the fulfillment to come. **"On the third day, I will raise thee up."**

Just as David and the people that are aligned with him are getting ready to be raised up, so is the Church of Jesus Christ in this new millennium going to rise. Some would scoff at the condition of society today and say that the revival of God is impossible for humanity as we know it. I believe that we are not only living in the greatest days of revival the earth has and will ever know, but I believe that this is final move of God, through the church, will be capstoned by the return of The Lord Jesus Christ for His Church. The Bible says that David and the people wept until they could weep no more. **Prayer must be more than your emotion released. Prayer must be our spirit in tune with God's spirit, saying and doing what God is saying and doing.** David knew this to be the secret to advancing from the deprived condition of the flesh to the deliberate, active blessing of God. Surely God wasn't in Heaven, giving up and crying.

One can react to distress in two different ways. A person will react either in their soul realm, or their spirit realm first. **The action of man is produced from the reaction of the soul or the spirit.** *If I react just from the soul to the manifestation, I'm in trouble. If I take it into my spirit first by faith, then I bring the moment into the captivity of my God given authority.* Spirit to soul, soul to body...This is the God-way of doing things. The righteousness of God not being revealed to the physical senses first, but to the spirit of man first. Any beginning in God's system must generate in the foundation of spirit. **Your renewed spirit is the God-part of you. That's where your God-results will always come from.**

The Bible says, in the 6th verse, that the soul of the people was grieved. Their answer therefore was the wrong answer. They spoke about stoning David. Their action began in their souls, not their spirit. David's reaction was different than theirs. The Bible says of David, that *he encouraged himself in the Lord.* As a matter of fact, David called for the Priest to bring him the ephod. **David would cover himself in the prayer garment of the Priest and received his instruction from God himself.** What was the spirit of God saying? Stone David? Give up? No. The reply of God was for David to *pursue the enemy, overtake the enemy and recover all.* That was God's answer! **Just because God shows a person the right way of doing things, does not necessarily mean that it is always followed.**

Not only was David a hearer of the Word, he was also a doer of the Word. The Bible says in verse 9, "So David went and he took 600 men with him." Amazing isn't it? *One proper God-decision made at the right time, and the same people that were ready to stone you, are now ready to fight with you.* **God will put a determination in your spirit that will be seen on your countenance.** They must have seen something in David's eyes that was different from what was in his eyes before prayer. In the opinion of this author, a warrior may have gotten off his horse, but a **priest got back on.** Everything God had revealed to David came to pass, because David moved past the intellect, emotion, and will of man. David's decision to trust in the

Lord brought the results necessary at that time.

The second example of David as Priest that I would like you to see is found later in David's life, in the 6th chapter of 2nd Samuel. David wanted to bring the presence of God back into the city center. There is not a single thing that a person could say was wrong with David's holy desire to get God into the center of Israel's life as a nation again. It was, without question, a "God thought." **Nevertheless, failure would mark David's first attempt at the restoration of God's presence.** Once again **a soulish attempt at a spiritual matter** would not meet the requirement of God.

The Bible says that when the oxen stumbled, the cart that was carrying the ark shook. When Uzzah tried to steady the ark with his hand, he was immediately struck dead. What insight here will help us understand the principle God would have us to know? The standard is simple. God has set patterns and laws. If these set patterns and laws are not followed, then **the futility of the flesh will reap a lesser result . . . and as in this case, perhaps even severe judgment based on prior instruction and accountability to that instruction.** Did the priest know how the Ark was to be transported? Absolutely. Had those instructions been passed on to the next generation? Evidently, not with enough of a sense of absolute urgency. The sons of Abinadab had made a grave mistake. **The sin of presumption will always be answered with the detail of the truth.** The name Abinadab in and of itself, is a key to that detail of truth.

The name **Abinadab** means... Father of a **vow**; my father is **noble**; my father is **willing**. You see, even though the bringing up of the ark was a noble gesture marked by a willingness of the people involved, it would still require the **vow** of the priest to make it happen. It would need to be **according to the pattern** that had always governed the ark's care and protection. The way of the priest had always been to bear the ark on their shoulders. Here, Israel is trying to transport the presence of God the way the Philistines did. **So many people today are looking for another way into the presence of God.** There are no short cuts into the holy place.

How brash this must have been to God, as the ark is being pulled around barbarically by the beasts of burden. What they were using to try and transport the ark, should not have even been a possibility to them. **What was empowering their error should have already been consumed in sacrifice! Oxen were for the altar, not for the**

ark. David and all of Israel would be taught a lesson from this event that would change their understanding of the ways of God forever. They would not learn to reverence the ways of God merely from the death of Uzzah alone, but it caused them to take a more intense look at what God truly represented to them as a nation.

They would learn how to operate in a correct manner in order to receive correct things.

David sent the ark to Obed-edom for three months to observe the ark. *While the ark was there, insight was given into divine blessing.* David was afraid on the day of Uzzah's death and wondered how he could ever get the ark into his city. He wasn't sure if the ark was a blessing or a curse. He would find out from three months of study that the ark was blessed. While the ark was at the house of Obed-edom, the entire household of Obed-edom was blessed. There was a visible difference in that city. **Blessing will always be visible.** David had to come to grips with the fact that they were the ones who had failed, not God. The 13th verse is the key..."he sacrificed the oxen and bore the ark on the shoulders of the priests," walking carefully six paces at a time, so that every seventh pace would be in the perfection of God's plan. **David had gone back and**

corrected his error in order to receive the correct thing
from God.

David danced before the ark of the Lord in a linen
ephod. He stripped himself of his Kingly garments and
bore the part of himself he loved the most…the Priest.
**David had not forgotten, but had remembered who he
was in his conduct that day.** He would be accused by Michal, Saul's daughter, of public humiliation. The Bible says
that she despised David in her heart when she saw him
dancing before the Lord in his linen garments. Michal was
always looking for her father Saul in David. She didn't understand what drove David from the inside. Her understanding of David's calling was weak, because she couldn't
see **the heart** of the King. Michal was distracted by her
prejudice that only saw the shell of the man, never seeing
the truest characteristic in his calling, the Priest.

The Bible tells us that because of Michal's inability to
see into the purpose of God's anointing on David, she was
unable to birth children until the day of her death. **The
barrenness of a lack of discernment, and actions that
accompany it, have been the tragic downfall of many in
the church throughout history.** Always looking for society's acceptance of the move of God. **Embarrassed by**

mindsets developed by their own pride. They mock the things of God through preconceived notions they've developed through improper teaching and rebellion that could never receive the Spirit of God.

God will never be mocked. He has chosen to use the foolishness of man to confound the "seemingly wise". God will bear his own burden, on the shoulders of his true Priests! David understood *he must pray as a Priest* if he were to embrace the approval of God for his people.

CHAPTER FIVE

HE SPOKE AS THE PROPHET

It would be David's ability to speak the heart of God effectively that would set him apart in history as one of the greatest Prophets the world would ever know. Any true leader would readily admit that often **the right decision is the hardest decision to make.** The easiest words to fall from human lips are those words that carry no power to affect the future. In the life of David, there would be few occasions where what he had to say carried no weight in regard to the stability of Israel's future. More often than not, an entire nation would hang on his every word. David would be better off to prophesy than he would to have a normal conversation among men. The anointing on David's life would not allow for hesitation. **He was called to be a vessel that God would need to be heard, as much as seen.**

A nation divided and a son dead, David is faced with the most important decision of his life. While as a normal man, he has every right to mourn the death of his own son. His responsibilities as the leader of God would allow him no time for grief. *An act of rebellion would be something that he would have the hardest time dealing with in his reign as king.* **Very often a decision avoided is an echo from the past, revisiting the inside of the halls of a heart that has gone unhealed.** Perhaps David's hesitation to address a nation is an indication of David wrestling with the notion that he somehow deserves to suffer for his past. **David must learn to separate mercy and justice** in the 19th chapter of 2nd Samuel. On a day that should have been marked only by celebration, the people of Israel that have been standing for the right by putting their own lives at stake, are made to feel that their efforts are in vain. *Due to David's inability to accept the full penalty of his son's rebellion, his judgment is temporarily clouded.* Undoubtedly, it is not an easy task for him as **the father of Absalom,** but it is here that he would have to consider his higher calling as **the father of Israel.**

The debate between personal family and spiritual ties has raged for centuries. *For some it is not hard to say that their family comes first.* **For others, those who are no longer their own, they understand that they will not have a family unless they put their higher callings first.** They understand that **they have been put on this earth for a divine purpose.** If that purpose goes unfulfilled, so will those things attached to them go unfulfilled. **Yes, family is of the utmost importance, and with that in mind the higher decision will benefit the truly closest to us.**

In the case of Absalom, it would be justice that he would receive through decisions that he made personally to separate from his own father's vision. **As for David, he would have to submit himself to a higher authority and not let his great love for his son interfere with his love for God himself.** David would not only have to choose mercy for the nation that day, but **he would also have to speak for mercy.** David was in a place of indecision in his chamber weeping, instead of standing over the gate speaking. Joab, the great General, motivates David to the awareness of the truth and his higher calling.

All of Israel had fled to their tents, undoubtedly in discussion of the position of David that so confused them. Rising to the surface of their imaginations must have been that they felt as though David loved Absalom, but did not share his heart for them. Joab was right in his assessment of the situation. Wisdom is always justified by her children, but **often wisdom does not carry the emotion of**

the problem in need of its correction. Wisdom will always give the right answer, but **wisdom will often leave a wake of the misguided behind it.**

Interesting that wisdom in the scripture is given an identity that is female. Most teachers today, male and female alike, tell us that it is **the male who will bypass the emotion** at the moment to cut to the chase of decision, and **the female who operates by the emotion first.** One must ask themselves the question if that is of the redeemed or unredeemed nature?

In the new covenant **there is neither male nor female by spiritual nature,** therefore **the veil of the flesh keeps both men and women from making the proper decisions in life.** The flesh of man, being no respecter of the spirit of man, fights hard to win out against the redeemed nature of both men and women in the Body of Christ.

Joab was not as emotionally attached to the decision that needed to be made that day. It was the son of David who had died. *David, Absalom's father, sat in his chamber between the gates.* He would have to be moved by God's Spirit. **Pulling back the curtain of his own flesh, David rises to his spiritual feet to command the hearts of the**

people who are waiting with baited breath to hear David speak. Whose father wouldn't stand over the gates of the city that day? Would it be the father of Absalom, or the father of Israel?

All of the people stopped their speculating and came out of their tents to listen to David. David would gather the elders at the gate and send them forth with his decision. **The words of David**, as recorded in the 11th verse of this chapter, **will encapsulate the power behind the man for all of time.** You have to see it. The kingdom had been divided under the rebellion of Absalom. *Those that went to their tents were also those who had anointed Absalom as their new king. They could be put to death by right of the law.* What would David do, and how would they be treated? This was a matter of life and death. David does not speak from his flesh, but from the spirit. **He speaks not as the king, but as the Prophet.** He prophesies! He refers to himself as **"king"** in the third person. "Why are ye the last to bring the king back to his own house?" The reason he refers to himself in this manner is because **he is outside himself here, operating in the higher calling. He says what no man could have released in the natural.** *He speaks God's will over the nation and not necessarily what his intention would have been.* It is a powerful example of the Prophet.

David submits to the God in him. David puts God before Absalom, knowing **it would be a seed he would need to sow for his future generations.** The Bible says David's words are so powerful, that **he bows the heart of an entire nation as if it were the heart of one man!**

CHAPTER SIX

HE WAS DEFEATED BY HIS FLESH

In all that we are allowed to see of David, we must consider that **he is a man born of flesh.** It is only the special empowerment that God gifts him with, that makes him great in our eyes. **Without God's gifting, he would just be one of many sons born to Jesse.** How important the flesh is to the masses today! How important is the flesh in the history of David?

Before you answer that question, let me ask you a question. **If his fleshly pedigree is so important, what is his mother's name?** Exactly! Most likely you could speak his father's name without hesitation. **The enemy would want us to focus on where we came from, instead of where we are now going. Our future is in the authority of Jesus Christ.** Like you and me, he would wrestle with his purpose, and at times question if he was making a difference. Can you imagine that? David would grow tired of his purpose, and place himself in a position of vulnerability.

Frailty is often defined by the strength of the individual, not the weakness. It was David's own strength that would be his downfall. Pride comes before fall.

It is when a man finds no necessity for God assistance that he places himself in harm's way. David relied on the strength of his own flesh and his own natural wisdom. All this, and still the Bible describes him as a man whose heart was fashioned after the likeness of the heart of God Himself! Many things would be said of David throughout his lifetime and after, **but who would ever have expected his greatest failure to be motivated by his own selfish desires.** The prophet of God comes to David to reveal his sin, in order for restoration to begin. The point God drives home through Nathan is that one lamb was stolen by a man who had many lambs.

The law broken first by David is disobedience. He should have been in battle with other Kings. That led to seeing what he never should have seen. **His second mistake would be covetousness.** David had made the common mistake of the flesh. **The flesh always wants what it has never had, and after it tastes the unknown, it still isn't satisfied!** Combine the attack of craving the unknown with being in the wrong place at the wrong time, and you have the potential for failure. **At a time when kings should be fighting, David stayed home.**

David could have avoided much pain in his life if he would have recognized his sin and made a decision to turn from it at its earliest stages. It was the murderous cover up, involving Uriah, that condemned David in the eyes of God. **It is hard to believe that God's psalmist is a murderer.** The Word of God allows us to follow David's life from a child, so that when this event takes place right before our eyes, we have a difficult time understanding how this could happen. It's a life lesson for every man and woman to glean from. Life lived out on this earth is not a simple thing. **If God does not remain in the priority of a human being, that human being will lose focus of all that is righteous.** Who could say what David was thinking. **It was David's own heart that had betrayed him.**

The very thing that we see is David's strength has become his weakness, when the element of God is removed from it. Like Adam, the first to fall to the temptation of the unknown, David would have to realize the absolute loneliness of the man who once walked close to God. **It is man's separation from God that will remind him of his need for God.**

There are many standards to receive from this part of David's life. First of all, **never make important decisions or drastic changes at a time when your body, mind, or spirit are not strong.** Exhaustion will always produce incorrect results, even in the lives of the best of men and women.

Secondly, there is a **deception of the flesh that will convince the mind that you can afford to allow things that you know aren't pleasing to God into your life.** *Pride will always ignore the standards of right living, excusing them as unnecessary and mindless.* The highest form of confusion is not in the blatantly wrong, but when part truth is embraced as all truth. **Deception in its highest form is when the one being deceived believes that they're actually in the right.**

Perhaps at the time, David thought it was acceptable to do what he did. Perhaps he felt he had earned the right to do what he did. At any rate, we know the end from the beginning, and can see in hindsight that this was not a repetitious practice or lifestyle for David. Thank God, David chose to repent of his sin and do right!

CHAPTER SEVEN
HE WAS LIFTED BY THE SPIRIT

Would there ever be restoration for David? The Bible is clear that if a man will turn away from a besetting sin, he will find forgiveness. **The key is the turning away from the sin;** the repentance. David would find his forgiveness under the law, even though it is an imperfect example in comparison to our covenant through Christ's blood.

David's prayer of repentance in Psalm 51 is a perfect shadow of a penitent spirit that finds the forgiveness of God in any age! Christ is faithful to bring a sincere heart to the Father, and the Father is faithful and just to forgive the sin and to cleanse from all unrighteousness. **David would regain his peace with God.**

From a broken heart this prayer is born. **Don't try to formulate from this prayer, for it is not calculated. These are words born in the spirit to birth a spiritual healing. David's spirit reaches out to the mercy of God, not His**

justice. If David got what he deserved through the penalty of the law, this would be his last prayer. "Have mercy upon me." David asks God to supernaturally wash him of his sin and the guilt of it. His appeal is also directly to God. "Against you only have I sinned." **Man may be wronged by another man, but man can only be forgiven by God.**

It's God's approval that beckons to the eternity in man. David mentions the "hyssop", or the bitter herb used by the Jews that dated back to the application of the blood over the door post and Israel's deliverance from Egypt. David was saying that he was torn up on the inside from his foolishness, and that the bitterness derived from his failure was teaching a lesson he would never forget. He would ask God to wash him on the inside by His blood. **This is a powerful prophetic prayer, saturated with divine insight into Calvary to come.** David tells God that he is embarrassed most of all to carry the weight of what he has done before the presence of God Himself. He asks God to hide his face from his sin. David has lost his love for the music, and wants it back. He asks God to **renew a joyful spirit in him** again and most of all **not to take the spirit of God from him** and remove him from his very presence. **David was given a unique seat in history with God.**

When David built God a tent to dwell in and brought His presence into the City of David, he had created for himself a venue that few had ever shared with God. God would only allow a handful of men in the earth to see Him as David did. This venue must have suffered interruption, for David asks for it back.

In the 91st Psalm, David declares that, "he that dwelleth in the secret place of the most high, shall abide under the shadow of the Almighty." **David had a view of God that few would ever share.** The shadow he referred to would be the actual shadow cast by the visible lighted presence of God that emanated from the ark of the covenant itself. That secret place was the holy place that he was allowed by God to enter into. It's a strong possibility that David may have even penned that 91st psalm with no need of a candle or lantern. **He would have the first-hand knowledge of the Shekinah presence of God.** "Cast me not away" has so much meaning here, when you understand what David stands to lose because of his sin. He knew the presence of God like no other of his time.

David was no stranger to giving to God. David remains one of the all time greatest givers in the history of the world. **David must have tried to get his forgiveness by way of the**

law, but felt no change on the inside because of his actions. His offerings and burnt sacrifices weren't working. Traditional approach isn't the answer here. **You can buy a pew for the church and fund the stain glass window project, but that's not what God wants from you.** "I bring my broken spirit and my contrite heart before you." David speaks from the heart to God and he tells him that he's broken down. Only God will be able to rebuild him back up to where he needed to be. **If you're reading this and are in need of God's forgiveness, ask him to help you get back on track with him right now. I've talked to too many people who allowed details to get in the way of their forgiveness. You must be forgiven and make heaven your destination after this life. There is no alternative.**

For David to come back to God in this manner is nothing short of incredible. To quote a great man of God, " I'd rather be a servant of God, than stoop to be a king." David knew that the earthly influences could be taken away from him, and that **all that mattered was that he was right before God.** David promised God that day that if He would clear his record for eternity, he would commit himself to be a giver of life and teacher of the ways of God.

Like Moses, David understood that it was far better to

know the ways of God than it was to merely benefit from the acts of God. The greater end of receiving is in the knowledge of God. Action is born from knowledge. **Knowledge is action's teacher.** David's prayer in the 51st Psalm would make him the teacher of Israel once again.

CHAPTER EIGHT

HIS GIFT WAS ADMIRED BY MEN

David's gifting was based on his purpose. **God had gifted David to rejoin Israel and lead them back to Jehovah.** God was using David to make Israel the great nation that God had intended for them to be all along. *A nation is only as great as the individuals that make up that nation.* **The strongest sense of David's gifting and purpose was the ability that his gift had to pull the gifting out of others around him.**

The people who rose to the top under David's leadership were the very ones that had to be lifted from the very bottom. The Word of God tells us that David's family and those who were in debt, distress and discontent we're the only ones to join him in the beginning. **Approximately 300 of the most discouraged people possible, and yet within them was the potential of Almighty God.** It would take the anointing and gift of David to pull it out of them. David was a man with a gift from God. His humanity is the key into the hearts of others. David may have been a leader of the past, but he remains an inspiration for leaders of the now and of the tomorrow. **David focused on the future of others, as well as his own life, that was to be pleasing to God.** David was the embodiment of a new day. His gift was full of promise, faith, and future.

The pace of our techno-society has led many astray today. Many think their destiny in God will come to them overnight without any labor. **Success in God is measured over a lifetime,** a good idea will never be enough. **Ideas are a dime a dozen.** Like David, **you must follow through to the end to fulfill your potential goals.** Working the ideas God gives you and your destiny will cost you something.

David's life is a portrait of satisfaction that is only acquired through intimacy with the one who controls the future. If you have a calling on your life, **the calling is only the time of your preparation.** *Gifts develop over time.* Many are called, but few are chosen. **The calling and the choosing are not one and the same.** The calling will lead you into your choosing. There can never be a choosing without first a calling. It is important to see the shepherd in David to understand the King. **Many had become frustrated with their lives, not because they have lost sight of their goals, but because**

they have lost sight of their God. Great men and women have quit too early. If your goals are not going to help build the Kingdom of God, then you may need to reevaluate your true purpose. *If a man or woman has experienced God in anyway, how can they live with themselves if what they do in this life is not making some impact for eternity.*

Like Absalom, **a conscious act of rebellion can only lead to destructive behavior.** There is still hope for the most destructive person out there. The grace of God will find you. When it does, embrace the moment. Positioning and timing are crucial in your pursuit of your destiny. Even when you are where you should be there is still a waiting on God that must take place before fulfillment comes. The only time David missed God is when he became intimate with the wrong people. *You can be friendly without being familiar.*

God's leaders must guard their gifts and anointing without falling into the trap of isolation. People will be attracted to your gift as a leader. **Make sure you use your gifts as a leader for the right reasons, always bringing glory to God.** David's gift inspired others that had given up on their own gifts.

There is a church out there waiting on a leader that no one else can even begin to appreciate. Gifts that have been thrown into the wayside will rise again to build for the Lord Jesus Christ. If we offer anything to this world, then it must come from God.

Let me encourage you to pursue God in your life and allow the gift of God to work in you like never before. This is not a transcription from a sixty-minute cassette of a better-than-average Sunday morning service. God is calling out to those who will be encouraged by the life of David to bring in a mighty harvest of souls. **Get a global perspective for the lost and don't let anything steal the joy of teaching transgressors His ways.** In all of David's failure, that would be the one thing he would cling to.

After over 20 years of ministry, **I have a better understanding of the grace of God. There is no extension of grace where there is rejection for rebellion, And there is no end to grace when there is a heart after His.** The gift of God's grace will turn the most hopeless cases into the mightiest men and women the world will ever know! Men admired King David, that is true. The greatest compliment of David would not be men's admiration, but the reproduction of this gift of God in others. The greatest compliment

to David is not what he took with him, but what he left behind.

E P I L O G U E :
FROM BOOK TWO

It would be Abraham who would lead us, as the father of faith, into a deeper revelation of what it is to hear from God and make the invisible visible. While most would try to retain riches by hoarding and conniving, Abraham would learn that with Jehovah God the secret to abundant increase was in the release. In order to truly see the hand of God made visible, you will have to let go of something precious in your life.

There will be a marked time of sacrifice on every road to divine purpose. God would ask Abraham to willingly offer up to Him the heir of his own body, Issac. There are some of us, who will not give God all of us, because there is a part of us we are not willing to let go. Your total release will bring God's total release into your life . . .

ABOUT THE AUTHOR

Dr. Terry Shuttlesworth is one of God's choice leaders in the world today. All who truly know him can see his love for God and consider him to be a Prophet reserved for the final harvest of souls on the earth.

In October of 2002, Dr. Shuttlesworth founded Dominion Christian Center in Virginia Beach. Virginia. The church is known as a mighty house of faith and miracles.

DCC has hosted guest ministries widely recognized as the most anointed and revered leaders of today.

Dr. Shuttlesworth has ministered fresh insight from the Word of God along with signs, wonders, and miracles throughout America and around the world for over thirty years.

STAY CONNECTED
with
Dr. Terry Shuttlesworth

Dominion Christian Center
2159 Lynnhaven Parkway
Virginia Beach, VA 23456
757.467.2400
www.DominionChristianCenter.com

Engage on Social Media

f /DCCVB   **🐦** @TShuttlesworth8

Watch live on Periscope!

📍 @TShuttlesworth8

NOTES

N O T E S

N O T E S

NOTES

www.ingramcontent.com/pod-product-compliance
Lightning Source LLC
LaVergne TN
LVHW041326080426
835513LV00008B/609

9780692657263